What others are sa

"Excellent work! I'm s ... 1's team and this was just what I needed to help me get started. Great job!!!" – A. C. *Ontario, Canada*

"Your book helped me with several issues. One thing that I think that all coaches and parents need to be aware of is that tee ball is a learning ground for not only kids but coaches as well. Just as a large majority of the kids have never played ball before, most of the coaches (including myself) have never coached before." – M. E. *New Jersey*

"Yippee! You saved the day with all the terrific information on coaching Tee Ball. We found your book after a desperate first practice. Desperate for ideas on where to start and where to go with these kids. Thanks for the wonderful compass you've given in "How To Coach Tee Ball Without Going INSANE." Super job!" – B. D. *Arkansas*

"You saved my life. I volunteered because no one else stepped forward and I am really enjoying coaching. Your tips will help me teach them the proper way to hit and throw so they will have a good time as they become more successful in mastering the game." – E. A. *Texas*

"Your book is great! As a youth sports director, I will be using it as an added resource for my coaches. It can be adapted for all levels of play and can fit into anyone's by-laws." – L. S. *Alaska*

"The information provided in your pages has caused me to change my approach in coaching this year. I've coached tee ball for four years; I wish I had this information earlier."
– B. J. *Georgia*

How To
Coach Tee Ball
Without Going
INSANE

How To
Coach Tee Ball
Without Going

INSANE

Robert Doss

Bullhorn Media Group
INSANEbooks Division

Published by:
Bullhorn Media Group
INSANEbooks Division
805 Westmoreland Lane
Cantonment, FL 32533 USA
Web Site – http://www.insanebooks.com
E-Mail – teeball@INSANEbooks.com

Library of Congress Catalog Card Number: 00-192695

ISBN: 0-9665944-0-1

Printed in the United States of America

1st Printing: 1998
2nd Printing: 1999
3rd Printing: 2001

CONTENTS

For my wife, Christina, who has always been a great sports parent and spouse, and to my two sons, Rob and Bryan, who made my dream of coaching my own children come true — it's an experience and memory I'll always treasure.

Also for Dr. Dayton Hobbs, whose vision brought us this game, whose perseverance has made it last, and whose personal values, morality, humility have given it direction and character.

FOREWORD

Managers and coaches of TEE BALL Baseball teams, as well as parents, whose boys and girls play in a TEE BALL Baseball program will benefit tremendously from this instructional book on TEE BALL Baseball written by Rob Doss.

Rob Doss spent a number of years coaching and managing TEE BALL Baseball in one of the finest programs I know, the Northeast Pensacola TEE BALL Baseball program. This fine program has always practiced the pursuit of excellence, and Rob was no exception as he has developed the practical drills, exercises, and approach to the game of TEE BALL Baseball that is set forth in this fine instructional manual.

As the Founder and President of TEE BALL Baseball, and the Director of the TEE BALL Baseball World Series held yearly at Gospel Projects Park in Milton, Florida, I can attest to the value of the instruction contained in this book. I have personally seen Rob Doss' product, the players themselves, who were trained under this system, and I can say that it works effectively.

I heartily recommend this book.

Dayton Hobbs
President
TEE BALL Baseball

ACKNOWLEDGMENTS

My first Tee Ball team was built around three returning players who knew how to play the game and four coaches, counting me, who did not. We finished with 5 wins and 14 losses, five times better than most expected we would do. My third and last season saw us finish with 18 wins and 1 loss, finishing second to a great team that beat us in a best-of-three playoff. At the end of my second season, I managed our league's five and six year old all star team and we finished third in a field of 26 teams. At the end of my third season, I was a coach for our league's Tee Ball World Series all star team. We won the championship and were chosen for the tournament's sportsmanship award by the tournament umpires — the first time a team had ever won both honors at once.

I learned a lot about Tee Ball during those three seasons and I learned them from some great people at the Youth Association of Northeast Pensacola (NEP) (Florida) ballpark. First of all, I'd like to acknowledge Billy Johnson and C. E. Mather, the park's Tee Ball Commissioners those three seasons who, while coaching teams of their own, adeptly organized the park's three Tee Ball leagues and 250 Tee Ball players. Their objectivity, fairness, and organizational skills were instrumental in our park's success during those three years. Billy and C. E. were very helpful to new managers and coaches and were great influences on me personally, and by extension, on my teams. Their influence was so positive that I later became President of the Park.

Parents play a huge role in the success that Tee Ball players and teams enjoy. From among a team's parents come the manager and coaches, sometimes the score keepers, team mothers, and always the fans. This game cannot be properly or effectively played unless the parents make it happen. I'd like to say thanks to those parents who made my teams successful: First, to the parents who helped me coach for their advice, help, and support during those three seasons:

Bill Parrish, Roy Stone, Bob Ulrich, Mark Fisher, Scott Smith, Lee Glaze, Paul Jones, and Michael Doss, and also to Willie Taylor who let me help him coach those Tee Ball World Series champions. A special thanks goes to my team's team mothers who skillfully kept us in business: Kim Ulrich and Toni Finger. Finally, I want to recognize the players who played for me and their parents for their cooperation and support during those seasons. The parents were the perfect fans and a coach's dream; their children were proof of good upbringing and were a pleasure to coach.

Chapter 1

INTRODUCTION

- History Of The Game
- Why This Game Can Be So Complicated
- The Game In Its Proper Perspective
- In a Perfect World...
- Let's Get Started

Tee Ball is a great game, but quite often, it's not until a parent begins managing or coaching, or has been around the game for a season that he realizes that there is more to this game than a bunch of kids dressed up like ball players chasing the ball and running the bases.

This is a sport that can produce young ball players who can make diving catches, throw runners out from their knees, and turn double plays. These magnificent feats do not occur unless they are effectively taught at home and coached on the ballfield. This handbook gives you what you need to begin helping children become good ballplayers so they can contribute to the building of the kind of team that can accomplish great things. Good luck!

History Of The Game

Hitting tees have been used by professional baseball players for more than fifty years to help them develop their swings for use against "live" pitching — the first hitting tees were made by Voit. The tee is great for practicing that "perfect swing" for players practicing alone and it's perfect for coaching hitting mechanics in a setting where the coach can pay close attention to every aspect of the swing.

It wouldn't surprise me a bit to learn that kids around the world have found ways to place baseballs or tennis balls atop some equipment resembling tees and making a game out of it for years. As you'll see in your experience in dealing with tee ball players, some of the neatest and most imaginative things come out of the minds of kids.

However, when it comes to laying credit for inventing the game of tee ball — that is, formulating rules, giving it organization and a name, and being the enabling force behind its development as a sport and not merely another backyard "hitting rocks with sticks" game, we go all the way back to 1960 and to Dayton Hobbs, then a thirty-eight year old elementary school principal from Bagdad, Florida near Pensacola. Dr. Hobbs had been coaching youth baseball since the 50's and took note over time of the little "fence grabbers" at the ballfield where his players worked out — you know, the kids who clutch and press their noses into the chain link fence to watch the big kids play. These were kids who, like we did, made heroes of their neighborhood stars and talked like real philosophers about who had "it" and who didn't. They'd run home, gather up whatever equipment they could find and play a game in the backyard, in the street, or in the vacant lot down the street.

Dr. Hobbs was coaching a group of 14 and 15 year old baseball players on their hitting when the co-mingling of baseball, hitting, tees, and the "let me try it" crowd of kids at the ballfield fertilized a creative seed in his mind and thus, he began work on creating Tee Ball Baseball — it seemed like the perfect game for players who had all of the desire but little of the physical development to play "real baseball."

Dr. Hobbs, who was also pastor of Grace Bible Church and President of the Santa Rosa Christian School in Milton, FL near the Naval Air Station at Whiting Field, went to work on developing rules for the game. A Navy chaplain from Whiting Field was one of Dr. Hobbs' first Tee Ball coaches (there were only two teams at first) and as they played, they refined the rules.

Dr. Hobbs soon began work on promoting the game, announcing that the game boasted some great features worth considering: "1) Inexpensive to play 2) Plenty of help available 3) Excellent parent cooperation 4) Doesn't require a large area to play the game 5) Minimum equipment required 6) Teaches basic baseball skills; and most of all 7) Boys and girls have loads of fun playing." His promotion efforts paid off as interest in the game grew and he was soon writing the first Official Tee Ball Baseball Rule Book.

His association with Navy people from Whiting and the growing popularity of the game in Pensacola, "The Cradle of Naval Aviation," led to a worldwide promotional forum he never anticipated. Soon, the game caught on at Navy bases in Japan and in Europe and across America until the success of the game led Dr. Hobbs to apply for a patent on the name and game of Tee Ball Baseball with the U. S. Patent Office in 1970, the same year the first annual Tee Ball World Series was held. His application met the stringent requirements for approval and won him recognition as the originator of the game of Tee Ball Baseball. He also won the patent on the four ounce bright orange official Tee Ball Baseball.

In the Official Tee Ball Rule Book, amended and published annually, Dr. Hobbs reminds us what the children already know: "that this is nothing more than a game of children's baseball." He admonishes managers and coaches "not (to) put pressure on the children, but attempt to teach them to play the game to the best of their ability while they enjoy it." The same guidance easily applies to Tee Ball parents.

Why This Game Can Be So Complicated

In one sentence, the reason this game can be so complicated is that many newcomers expect Tee Ball to be just like baseball. But it isn't. The game was created as a way of introducing young children to the game of baseball so they could enjoy this great sport while developing baseball skills and sportsmanship at a pace they could handle.

The official Tee Ball Baseball rule book published annually in Milton, Florida provides a very comfortable atmosphere in which these objectives can be met, as do many other rule books published throughout the world. In the Tee Ball Baseball rule book, there are provisions built in to suit local needs for younger players. The official rules of baseball generally apply to Tee Ball Baseball, but the fact that the ball is placed on the tee and hit while stationary demands that there be a re-balancing of the relative advantages enjoyed by the offense and defense.

Because a fairly uncomplicated game like baseball has been adjusted to accommodate young children, the game is packed with judgment calls for the umpires and the need for managers, coaches, players, and parents to learn the ins and outs of a game they might not otherwise recognize. The failure of coaches and parents to understand the game of tee ball has hurt many children by denying them the benefit of meaningful well-developed training right from the start. I have heard from dozens of coaches and parents who have told me that they wished they'd known more about the game earlier. Unfortunately, a late start in a game like tee ball or baseball typically means the player won't make up the difference until the next season when he can get a better start.

Since the game can get complicated at times, managers, coaches, and parents need to put some thought into how they intend to teach their players the game. Tee ball players generally range in age from 4 to 7 years, with some getting as young as 3 and some girls as old as 8. Many of us learned baseball long ago and have long since forgotten what it was like to see baseball through a child's eyes. This gap tends to produce one of two outcomes in coaches and parents.

On one hand, some describe the game in adult terms, not appreciating the fact that these kids don't know what it means to "step in the bucket" or "take an extra base" until someone tells and shows them and they've had a chance to practice it a lot.

On the other hand, some underestimate the importance of well-developed tee ball skills and remain silent to the extent that they teach them nothing about the game. Some parents make so little of their children's athletic endeavors to the point that the children become incredibly awkward and unprepared on the field because they are "oh-so-cute," uninitiated to the learning environment the coach is there to maintain. You can teach these youngsters to "get in the dirt" and "turn two." Of course, you can anticipate less than perfect execution, but it's fun to watch them learn and attempt these skills. It is utterly satisfying to see them do it right, even if it's only once in a while, but you'll find that if you can get them to be successful a few times they soon gain confidence and consistency.

As you might expect, you have to have a lot of patience and perseverance to manage, coach, and teach a group of tee ball players. When you lose your patience with your players, they can see it on your face. Of course, as part care-giver, part coach, part teacher, and part parent figure, you need to motivate your players through the use of a variety of leadership tools. Use them prudently and judiciously. Remember that this game, like any new game, can be complicated for them too.

I used to be a U. S. Marine helicopter flight instructor and ultimately became a standardization pilot — an instructor's instructor. I used to tell new flight instructors that the trick to being a great flight instructor was knowing how to present the same material dozens of different ways. Each of those deliveries is like a key, and when you can walk into the cockpit with a pocket full of those keys, you improve your student's chances of learning the material. The same principle applies to coaching: The likelihood that you will succeed as a coach with only one way to describe or teach a skill is very poor.

Successful coaches are those who can take physical challenges and use analogies and common visual imagery to establish an intellectual and cognitive connection with their players. For tee ball players, these images are best when they are a bit dramatic: point the belly button toward the part of the field where you want to hit the ball, make your arm like an elephant's trunk when throwing, and point the button on your cap toward the direction from which the ball came, for instance.

Parents are almost uniformly surprised at how capable their children are at learning a sport and developing athletic skills. In some cases, this surprise is preceded by skepticism. Great coaches do not allow this skepticism to deter them from formulating success for their teams and players. Obviously, it takes a lot of work at home, practice on the field, and patience from coaches and parents. In any case, diligence, persistence, and the proper perspective will simplify the complexity of this game.

The Game In Its Proper Perspective

As managers, coaches, and parents grow in their understanding of the game and try their hands at teaching young players the game, they come to realize that there is much more to properly coaching a Tee Ball team than simply chaperoning kids with gloves on their hands. They learn, some sooner than others, that these children bring with them all of the elements that favor the coach in his role as teacher. It is an incredible waste of an opportunity and a great injustice if parents and coaches don't do their best to teach their players as much as they can.

How do they do this? How far do they go? Is it reasonable to expect 5, 6, and 7 year old children to learn to stop the ball when it's hit to them? How about catching fly balls? And throwing the ball to the right base? Should they be drilled on throwing accurately? Should they be taught to hit properly? Does it really make any difference if the players develop terrible bat swings or that they don't get in front of the ball when they field it? Let's look a little further. Knowing that your players are going to slide into bases,  should they be taught the right way to slide, or should they be allowed to do whatever they want to do? Most parents and coaches agree that these things should be taught, particularly when they learn that the game is made safer by quality comprehensive instruction, but few progress further because they either lack the knowledge to teach the right thing or they're reluctant to get too deeply involved in the game, or both.

You see, this is such a difficult issue for many because parents and coaches often confuse perspective with commitment. They don't know where the line is between taking their responsibilities seriously and taking an excessively aggressive approach to the game. They're uncertain whether they have lost their perspective or upheld their commitment when they take the time to develop their players' skills with a lot of practice and drills. That's why some leagues don't keep score — they're concerned about the outcome. I recommend parents and coaches remember two important things about Tee Ball: First of all, they should remember that Tee Ball is only a game. Secondly, they should remember that understanding that Tee Ball is only a game is not a good excuse to avoid teaching their players about winning, losing, sportsmanship, gamesmanship, and "gutting it out."

Ask a coach why he doesn't teach and drill his players on basic baseball skills and he'll usually tell you, "We're not that serious about the game here." Well, why aren't they? And why does the chief complaint people have about youth athletics usually have something to do with someone taking the game "too seriously?" Many attribute this problem to the competition, but as far as I'm concerned, the problem, insofar as it *is* a problem, is actually caused by poor behavior by adults who should know better. My children have played in both, competitive Tee Ball leagues where score was kept and outs were counted and so-called "non-competitive" Tee Ball leagues where there was none of that. However, based on my own experience as a parent and coach, I can confirm that the one thing that is common to both types of leagues is the presence of a relatively few obsessive adults who always seem to find ways to have a problem with the umpires, the coaches, the parents, the score, and so on. Precautions such as changing the rules of the game and not keeping score don't prevent these problems, they simply provide them different grounds on which to surface. The problem is not that the game is taken too seriously — the problem is that we adults can tend to lose our perspectives.

My team lost the fifteenth game of my first season as a coach by 40 runs. That ran our record to 1 win and 14 losses. Humiliating, right? Nope. Most of my players didn't know the difference. Kids place a premium on what their coaches and parents emphasize. At the end of that game, we emphasized appreciating the skill and teamwork the other team demonstrated and noticing that they obviously played hard and had fun along the way. Our kids were smart — they knew the other team was really good and they wanted to be like them. We took satisfaction in recognizing that our own players played hard and had fun, and that they were making great progress as they went — some day they'd blossom. However, after the game a parent approached me and told me that one of the other parents had been making a fuss in the bleachers over our team's lack of success. I phoned that parent and asked him if there was something we needed to talk about and after a while, we got down to it. He said that he was tired of being humiliated and he was tired of seeing his kid humiliated.

I didn't pull any punches. I told him that if his kid was humiliated, it was probably because his father was focusing on the wrong things. We had a team that was not good enough to beat the good teams and nothing we did at practice and nothing I said at the games was going to change that. Our job was to capitalize on our opportunities and not to place unrealistic expectations on our team. As it turned out, our last four games of the season were with teams nearer to our own caliber and our kids did fine. In fact, we won those four games, the kids loved it, and we did it without compromising the principles we had maintained all along. Unfortunately, there was grumbling in the bleachers again and, of course, I made a second phone call to the same parent I had called four games earlier. This time his complaint was that he didn't like having his kid play on a team where winning was everything. What do you do?

The fact is that it's essential that everyone take the game seriously — coaches, parents, umpires, and children. Taking your responsibilities as a manager or coach seriously means that you don't lose your head during a close game. It means that you teach your players as much as is reasonable and give them every opportunity to become good enough to have bright moments in games. It means that you teach them how to lose gracefully after a tough game and it means that you teach them how to be generous and polite when they win. It means that you teach them about teamwork and cooperation and it means that you help them become disciplined enough to do what you taught them to do. It means that you teach them to play aggressively and ambitiously, but it also means that you don't win at all costs. It means that if your team is a little short of talent that you do as much as you can with your team and your individual players anyway. In Tee Ball, there's always something to be successful at.

A coach's perspective is not blown simply because he insists that his players not hit pop flies or because he has a word for them when they make an error of concentration on a routine play. His perspective is blown when he expects players to perform skills in games that they have not first mastered in practice, or when he handles a situation on the field in anger without regard for the example he sets for the players. In my opinion, he has also blown his perspective when he does not attempt to train his team to standards of excellence. Realize that I didn't say that he has blown it when his team doesn't *achieve* excellence; I said that he has failed when he doesn't try and doesn't encourage his team to try to accomplish what they can. Regardless of the won-lost record at the end of the season, if you take your responsibilities seriously and keep things in perspective, you will build a team of winners.

When parents don't take the game seriously they don't work with their kids at home, cheer for them in the bleachers, and have them to practice and games on time.

When umpires don't take the game seriously they don't hustle to see the whole play so the great plays can be properly recognized and rewarded and they don't ensure the rules of the game are enforced so that orderly play and a proper learning environment can be assured.

When the players don't take the game seriously they don't learn and they don't attain the physical and mental development this game is designed to give them.

You see, not taking the game seriously enough is at least as damaging as taking it "too seriously."

Let me set one thing straight right here at the beginning: I hate to lose at ANYTHING; however, I know how to take a setback and turn it into an opportunity. How many Baseball Hall of Famers failed in more than 60% of their attempts to reach base safely? Success has its sweetest taste when it has risen out of failure.

Coaches should never quit on their players or their team, parents should never quit on their children, and players should never quit on themselves — regardless of how bad things appear.

In A Perfect World...

In a perfect world, everyone would maintain the proper perspective and coaches would be flawless in their management of people, time, and material resources... but they're not. Parents need to keep their eyes open and speak up when they have a question or a problem with what is happening on their child's team. It has long been my sense that as long as people communicate, many problems will be resolved before they see the light of day. Coaching a winning team brings with it a set of responsibilities different from coaching a losing team, but no more or less important to the children on the team. These responsibilities are difficult to identify sometimes, especially on the first pass. Parents need to help their coaches out and be a good influence and assistance to them. Parents and coaches need to do their best with the children, but remember that this is not a perfect world, and that by cooperating, the task is much easier.

Let's Get Started

Since the game can get complicated at times, parents and coaches need to get a good start if they are to make a meaningful contribution to the children's understanding and preparation for the game.

I must confess to an abundance of naïveté during the two years that I watched the game and for much of the first season that I coached it. The old adage that "I wish I knew then what I know now" certainly applies to me, and as I've already mentioned, from the letters I've receive, it apparently applies to a lot of other people too. To be honest, I wish I knew more back then so I could have played a larger personal role in the development of my children during those critical early playing days. As you continue reading this booklet, parents, please remember this encouragement to be a great help to your child off the field, then turn him over to the coaches on the field. When he's on the field, be the best fan in the stands and be unflinching in your support of him and his team. With your help, he will enjoy tremendous progress.

Managers and coaches, set and seek whatever goals you can reasonably set for your players, but don't tarnish your achievements and theirs by failing to have fun... and ensuring your players do the same.

Chapter 2

MANAGERS & COACHES

- Where Do They Find The Managers & Coaches
- What's Their Job?
- They Have To Understand The Rules
- Tee Ball Baseball Rules
- Coaches And Their Kids

Tee Ball managers and coaches are not professionals. Typically, they are somewhat reluctant volunteers who give in to the opportunity to coach their children while the stakes are fairly low. They discover along the way that they have signed on to a huge responsibility and they're expected to have at least some sort of clue about the game.

Where Do They Find The Managers & Coaches?

My eldest son played Tee Ball two years before I began coaching the game and I had absolutely no idea what it took to try to bring a team together. I watched every practice and every game I could, but still had no real appreciation for how his coach got his job or how he went about his business.

I became a Tee Ball manager and coach the same way a lot of people do — I told someone that it would be neat to coach my kid some day — I must have said it one too many times to one too many people. I received a phone call shortly before the season began and was asked to manage a team that had some problems with managers and coaches in the past. I hesitated because my work schedule was so rigorous and it meant having my eldest son change teams in his last year of Tee Ball. I agreed to take the job and found out that I was left with only three players from the previous season. That didn't really bother me too much until I saw what all of the other teams were bringing along. I had to build a team of 13 players practically from scratch and I wasn't sure how to begin. Fortunately, the park's Tee Ball Commissioner, the man who had asked me to manage, was more than helpful. He managed a team of his own and was very generous with advice on how to practice and what to practice on. Unfortunately, I'm sure I missed three-quarters of what he had to say because it was so foreign to me. The things I did follow were very difficult to put into practice because I didn't really have a core of player and coaching experience to build upon. I asked every parent on the team to volunteer as much as they could and tried to find three parents to serve as full-time coaches. I was lucky enough to find some great help.

Almost anyone you can talk into coaching tee ball has at least played some kind of ball before. However, very few will have ever had prior coaching experience. Coaching is much different than playing and having been a good player is no assurance that you will be a good coach. A coach must possess certain qualities. Now, I choose the word "qualities" carefully because so many coaches simply have "characteristics." A coach has to be a good teacher, he has to be patient, he has to be confident and decisive, he has to be nurturing when his players get hurt or make mistakes, and he has to be able to get as much as he can out of his players without going too far. Managers don't have to look for coaches that fit this description, but they do need to find people who will be willing and able to adopt these qualities and adapt to the environment the manager sets. If they're lucky, as I was, their coaches will be good because the parents of the kids on their team are good.

Coaches, remember that your assistant coaches will probably know much less about the game than you do. They're parents just like you. You have to work very hard to develop in your coaches an appreciation and consensus for your goals for the team and the strategies for achieving them. Regardless of what they do or don't know about the game, it's very important that they respect the manager's position. There is no way a team will achieve its best when the coaching staff is at odds with itself. There are hundreds of ways to coach a team; assistant coaches must recognize this and hitch their wagons to the team that the manager brings, providing meaningful and discrete advice and dissent as they go.

Since assistant coaches are normally new to tee ball coaching, managers often have to help them learn how to coach. One good way to break a coach in and get him into the flow of working with players is to practice base running with him coaching a base. It can be very frustrating for him to try to get a 5-year old player to understand when to slide, or when to run through 1st base, or take two steps on a fly ball. Coaches quickly get over their reluctance to speak up when the runners don't execute their instructions the way they want them to.

What's Their Job?

The manager is the single point of contact between the team and local park officials. Most of the time, the manager also assumes the role as the head coach. Many parks aren't funded or staffed sufficiently to keep teams from having to raise funds to keep the park in business, so there might be obligations that the team needs to meet such as concession duty, score keeping, fund-raising, field preparation, and more that the manager has to coordinate. The manager simply coordinates these efforts and counts on the participation of the players' parents — with their cooperation, he can devote more time to his actual coaching duties.

They Have To Understand The Rules

Tee Ball is played just like baseball except for the rules that are intended to balance the advantage the batter enjoys as a result of him hitting a stationary ball off the tee. That one facet of this game presents angles peculiar to Tee Ball that must be examined, understood, and communicated to coaches, players, and parents. I've been in games where parents who've been around the game for a few years heckle umpires and coaches because of calls and decisions they've made and the only mistake that was made was that the parent didn't understand the game. For instance, Tee Ball Baseball has specific rules about the stoppage of play after the ball is hit. If you don't know those rules, this game can be very frustrating. Tee Ball parents normally count on their coaches to help them understand the rules of the game, but I can tell you that coaches often do not fill this gap — many times, the rules are new to them too. Once you're finished reading this booklet, pick up a copy of the official Tee Ball Baseball rules and read them from cover to cover — you'll end up very well-informed and prepared. If you don't know your way around Official Baseball Rules, read up on them as well. The more you know about the game, the better off your children will be (it might also keep you from pressing the umpire too far on a judgment call).

Tee Ball Baseball₍ₐ₎ Rules

As I've already said, my children have played in a couple of different tee ball programs under different rules. The various national affiliates often have their own rules, but frankly, those rules tend to appear to treat tee ball as a bit of an afterthought — not a lot of imagination and gamesmanship went into the creation of some of them.

The best rules I've seen for playing tee ball are those written and updated annually by the affiliate that created the game in the first place, Tee Ball Baseball, Inc., headquartered in Milton, Florida. Tee Ball Baseball, Inc. sanctions leagues that desire to franchise with them and can be contacted at the address noted inside the front cover of this book.

A sampling of the rules contained in the Tee Ball Baseball rule book follow:

The Tee Ball Baseball official rule book calls for 45' baseline distances and 115' to 125' fence distances (125' for championship play). Around home plate, there is a 10' arc — if a batted ball fails to go beyond this arc, it's a foul ball. The pitcher's "mound" is a circle with a radius of 5', the center of which is 35' from the tee (the pitcher must stay within this circle until the ball is hit). The batter's box is 5' long and 3' wide. It is placed 6" off of home plate with 2' extending forward from the center of home plate (and 3' extending backward from the center of the plate).

The ball is the 4 ounce TB-100 orange ball produced by Worth Sports Company (it's 1 ounce lighter than a regulation baseball). The bat is not less than 24" nor more than 27" in length and the barrel is not greater than 2-1/4" in diameter. Batters, runners, and catchers wear batting helmets.

The game length is 6 innings. Starting lineups consist of 10 players — the 10th player is an additional outfielder. There is a mandatory participation rule: 3 full innings on defense and at least one turn at bat. A team on offense has 3 outs or 10 batters, whichever comes first, per inning.

There is no infield fly rule and no bunting, chopped swings, or any other kind of swing that is intended to "kill" the batted ball. Three strikes and you're out and three fouls on the third strike and you're out too.

The batter hits the ball and the defense does its level best to get him out with a good baseball play (no running half way across the field to make a one-man play). Once the ball is hit and cleanly fielded, the umpire blows a whistle. The whistle means that the player can advance no further than the base to which he is headed. The play is ended when the players are on base and the ball is rolled into the catcher. No defensive team in its right mind rolls the ball into the catcher until the players are forced back to their bases.

Coaches And Their Kids

The most difficult thing a coach has to do is see the 12 players on the field who are not related to him. We tend to be very tough on our own kids without giving them the consideration we give the other players. If you can do it, try to be a coach on the field and a parent off the field, and get your fellow coaches to do the same. Impartiality (and avoiding excessive impartiality) is essential to success.

Chapter 3

WORKING WITH PARENTS

- What Should Parents Expect Of Their Coaches?
- Do The Coaches Need Parents' Help?
- Parents As Fans

A coach can tell a lot about the kind of player he's getting by looking at the parents of the player. It has been my contention that I started with the makings of a good team because my players' parents were good. This proposition proved true during my three regular seasons and it was true during the two all star seasons I coached. Good parents make it possible for a coach to do a good job with his players.

What Should Parents Expect Of Their Coaches?

Parents can complicate or simplify a coach's job. They tend to know exactly what they want their kid to get out of his ball playing experience and this can translate into hostility toward the coach if those goals are not met or into great esteem if they are. Some see their kid as a fledgling big leaguer who needs only time to make the big time, provided he gets good coaching. Others just want their kids to have fun. They see Tee Ball as a game where a bunch of cute little kids dressed up as ballplayers hit the ball, chase the ball, and run the bases. This is quite a range of expectations for a coach to try to satisfy — and he can't do it. Before we get too far into the details of the game, let's talk about the need for coaches to set goals and communicate them to the parents.

As my first season got underway, I held a parents' meeting during which I described my philosophy, the practice routine, and so on. Having understood the conditions under which I became the manager, I didn't want to pick up where the previous manager left off. I told them that I intended to practice for about an hour or an hour-and-a-half twice a week, three times if they really wanted to. I told them that we would be budget-conscious when it came to uniforms, and that our goal was to make a team and have fun. I didn't see it right away, but I had a friend who sat on the board of directors at the park who incredulously asked me if it was true that these were my plans. I said yes, and he gave me a quick lesson on the realities of coaching at that park. It seems that a couple of parents were disappointed that their kids weren't going to get more out of this season as indicated by my plans for practice and the uniforms. In reality, I just

38

didn't want to alienate the parents and would have loved to approach the season more aggressively. Well, I had another parents' meeting and the long and the short of it was that we practiced four times a week, bought nice uniforms, and the parents were satisfied with the approach. My approach toward the players remained the same; it was the involvement and the investment that changed. (Of course, we still lost fourteen of our nineteen games that season!)

As Park President, I always encouraged parents in the strongest possible terms to do everything they could to be the kind of ball parent that would make their children easy to coach. I told them that once you determine that their coaches have the "qualities" they can accept, remembering that no one is perfect and that hindsight is, as the say, "20-20," they needed to give their coaches the room they needed to do a good job.

Do The Coaches Need Parents' Help?

Coaches need the assistance of their players' parents. I found that parents are normally willing to help out if they aren't too busy and they tend to learn that the more they participate in the operation of the team, the more they also stay in touch with the challenges coaches encounter as they try to build their team.

Parents As Fans

There can be three hundred people in the stands and three coaches shouting during a game, but the one voice a player hears is his own mother's. This isn't a problem until the coach tells the player to stop and she yells for him to go. The only thing a coach can do about this is tell the parents how tough it is to communicate with the players when there are conflicting instructions on the field. Learning to be a good fan is tough too, but it's also very important.

Once I got my confidence as a manager, I saw the need to make sure I got control not only of the happenings on the field, but also activities in the bleachers. As difficult as it is for a coach to treat his kid as just another player, it's even more difficult (and rarer) to see a parent in the stands who is just a good fan. Most parents see only one kid. They see every mistake he makes, they hear what the coach tells him, they see their child sitting on the bench, and they see (or think they see) their coaches cause him to make outs. Coaches need to communicate with their players' parents and let them know that it's important for them to be good fans and supportive of the whole team. Also, coaches need to show parents that as the coaching staff places demands on the children, they will be fair to them — it's not necessary for parents to glare at their kids, or to communicate disapproval through the field fencing. A well-coached player will be aware of his mistakes without looking into the bleachers for confirmation of them from his parents. One of the best ways for coaches to show parents that they will do the right thing with players is to do the right thing with their own children.

I sat in the bleachers to watch a Tee Ball game one season and listened to a parent tell her friend (who was apparently new to Tee Ball) that "the refs are okay, but the coaches don't understand that these kids are only 7 years old and can't always make the plays they want them to make." I have to confess right away that her credibility was suspect because she called the umpires "refs," but I took a wait-and-see attitude nonetheless. I saw nothing odd from the coaches, but a little while later I did have the opportunity to watch that lady's son make a fielding error in left field. How did I know it was her son? I could tell because as soon as the ball got past him, she came unglued and stayed that way for several minutes. I was alarmed at how she badgered and belittled her son without shame. I've seen good coaches and bad, but I can say that I've never seen one get on and stay on a player like she did with her son. The fact is that 7 year old players can make good plays, but they will not do it consistently or when the heat is on when they have the type of fan support like that young man had.

Chapter 4

THE PLAYERS

- What Do They Know?
- Equipping Players
- Left-Handed Or Right-Handed?
- How Responsive Are They At This Age?
- The Value Of A "Spirited" Player
- Watch Them Mimic
- Can Girls Play This Game?

The level of performance you expect of your players will directly influence the level of output you receive from them. If you're aware of what they already know when you start out and have some concept of what they are capable of, you can come much closer to understanding the skills you can expect to develop in them.

What Do They Know?

Coaches have to assume that even if a player's parents have been teaching him to throw, catch, and hit at home, he probably has not been taught how the game is properly played. I'm not going to say that it's entirely the coach's fault if the player moves on and hasn't learned how to play ball, but I will say that one should presume that a player will not learn the game unless his coach teaches him. Understand that at some point once he leaves Tee Ball, his next coach will ask him who his coach was the previous season. You want to make sure the player says your name proudly and that his new coach sees your efforts effectively invested.

Parents mean well when they teach their kids at home. However, often neglected along the way are the good fundamentals you want them to put into play. As they say, you can't teach old dogs new tricks — the same goes for the kid who has learned a ball skill fundamentally incorrectly. Once a player adjusts to fielding balls off to the side of his body or turning his head on a grounder, it's hard to change him, even though his lack of success indicates he should try something else.

Equipping Players

If it weren't for the memory of how I equipped my own child for his first season of Tee Ball, I would have found some humor in some of the things I saw when new players showed up on the field for the first time when I was coaching. Here are some tips that will save parents money and ensure that they put the right gear on their players the first time:

Ball Glove

Of course, parents are going to get into the inevitable color discussion with their children. My children have owned black gloves and regular rawhide-colored gloves. However, they have never owned a green, red, orange, or purple glove, nor have they ever owned a plastic glove. The glove will need to be larger than you think it should be. A twelve-inch glove is normally not too large. Normally, a player who can't handle a twelve-inch glove probably can't catch with a smaller one either. Parents should get their child a leather glove (stay away from plastic), read the instructions that come with it and break it in, break it in, break it in. When they break it in, they need to make sure the palm of the glove has the same breaks that the palm of your hand has. In other words, they need to take care that the glove is not broken so that it closes only at the thumb or at the little finger. Children should learn the importance of taking care of their glove early — they should be taught how to take care of the glove and keep it dry. There are a number of glove treatment products on the market and they are typically a good investment. Of course, everyone follows the directions on the package, but in case the warning slips by, take care not to oil the laces of the glove unless you like tying a lot of knots.

Shoes

Parents should anticipate that their children will need a new pair of shoes every season. They shouldn't get tennis shoes; they should get spikes that are approved for league play and try to stay away from getting something "cute" with funny little cartoon characters that will not work out well on the ballfield. Tee Ball shoes do not need to be "top-of-the-line," but should still be properly fitting and provide sufficient support for athletic wear.

Batting Gloves

I'm a bit old fashioned, I guess, but I don't want my players wearing a bunch of jewelry and other things that aren't directly related to their performance on the field. With this said, I don't look at batting gloves as being extraneous equipment. The glove doesn't have to be the top-of-the-line glove because kids don't wear it out as much as an adult might. Should you get him one glove or two? When I play ball, I use two, but I know a lot of people who use just one on the bottom hand as they hold the bat.

Tee Ball Bats

Parents often make their most costly equipment mistakes when they buy bats for their children. First of all, find out what the bat length, weight, and barrel diameter restrictions are for your league.

Check the official rule book for a complete description. With the legal limitations in mind, coaches and parents should make sure their child can effectively handle the bat. Keep in mind that there is a right way and a wrong way to swing a bat, and unless the player's bat is light enough for him to handle effectively with a fundamentally sound swing, it's too heavy. On the other hand, understand that he should swing as heavy a bat as he can effectively handle so he can deliver as much power to the ball as he can. The proper swing is described later in this handbook and provides a good basis for determining the right bat for your player.

Water Bottle

Parents should invest in a non-spill plastic water bottle for their children. Children sweat and dehydrate just like adults do and their performance falls off considerably as a result. Have them take a water bottle with them to practice and the games. If a child or team is uncharacteristically lethargic and you're left scratching your head over it, look at their water intake. Water wins games.

Left-Handed Or Right-Handed?

I don't have any secrets for figuring out whether a player should throw and bat left or right-handed. If you spend some time watching the player when he handles a ball, over time he will develop a preference for which hand to throw with.

Most people bat right-handed if they throw right-handed and vice versa, but in reality, people can learn to hit either way.

When players begin to hit pitched balls, they should be coached to keep both eyes on the ball, but their tendency is to turn their heads slightly so that one eye is closer to the pitcher than the other. Ensure your tee ball players address the ball with both eyes and don't let one eye dominate over the other. If they get into the habit of allowing one eye to dominate over the other in tee ball, they might suffer a great disadvantage at the plate in later years if they aren't corrected. Still, players will tend to turn their heads slightly and the "dominant" eye theory of hitting — that everyone has a dominant eye and that this eye should be nearest the pitcher — might apply. I honestly don't know whether this theory holds any water — there seem to be a lot of successful switch-hitters in the world who overcome that "dominant" eye quite well.

Ensure your child doesn't develop a cross-handed swing. As the batter addresses the batting tee with the bat, one of his shoulders will be closer to the pitcher than the other. The hand that's connected to the arm that's connected to that forward shoulder should be on the bottom as the child grips the bat. Again, more information on hitting follows in Chapter 7.

How Responsive Are They At This Age?

By now you're probably wondering if you can make it happen. Let me tell you that players will surprise even their own parents when they see the rate and degree of mental and physical development the children undergo during the season.

Remember as you go along that in spite of all that you do and all the time you invest, some players will not get as good as you would like them to be. If you find that's the case, let it be. Keep working with the player and help him develop at his slower pace; it might surprise you when he finally comes into his own. Be patient with him. I was just as proud of the slower player who kept working as I was of the others because he had overcome the overwhelming temptation to give up. Instead, he worked and worked and finally stood in there against the fly ball or threw the runner out at second base because of that determination. The joy of having a great won-lost record in my final season was vastly overshadowed by the fact that all of our players were making plays in the field, at the plate, and on the base paths by season's end. Players who were once content to let the ball roll to the fence before picking it up were charging the ball and throwing runners out at second base...just like we practiced.

Some kids do not respond well to their own parents so there is no reason for their coaches to expect that they will get through to them either. With that said, I've seen kids who ruled the roost at home but responded very well to their coaches on the field. Coaches should never assume that just because they want something out of their players that they will get it strictly on the basis of their charm and mass appeal. They have to rely on feedback to create, elevate, and sustain performance. Remember that these kids have their pride just like we do and that your negative feedback counts to them. Use it discretely and thoughtfully.

On the other hand, lavish the positive feedback on them and you'll be surprised at the return. It was not uncommon for me to call a timeout to march out onto the field, call a huddle, and tell a player that he had just made the most awesome play I'd ever seen. When we got three outs during an inning we made a huge fuss over it. I made a personal point not to punish errors or outs. However, there were many laps run around the field when fundamentals were not adhered to (whether he caught the ball or got on base or not), or when the player didn't hustle to first base, or when the player didn't do what his coach told him to do. Again, we didn't make a big deal of it — it was just part of the arrangement. Your failure to address a fundamental problem provides implicit support of it and invites a repetition down the road.

The great thing about young tee ball players is that they will generally perform the way you want them to if you don't give it a second thought. Kids are funny. They can sense the slightest indecision or hesitation on your part and are reluctant to follow you to the water fountain if you don't look and act like you know what you're doing, and back it up with performance. However, if you show them how good they can be and don't let them settle for mediocrity, they will astound even themselves. This does not mean that you ride them and badger them into performing. You have to inspire them and make them want to do what you want them to do. If you can show them a couple of players on the team who do it right, that's all of the proof they need to show that they can do it too.

Along that same line, if you can get each player to show the team how quickly he grasps the new skill you taught in a team huddle, he will always have a personal standard to refer to. I used to say something like this: "Okay, Johnny, show everybody what you look like when you're waiting for someone to hit the ball to you." Johnny would show everyone and he'd do a fine job so I'd tell Adam to give it a try, then Kristine. By the time we were finished, we'd shown everyone how good it looks to hold a good defensive stance and several players had received personal attention and reinforcement for their efforts. I didn't have to beat the kids up and they still learned exactly what was expected of them. They do want to look good and perform properly if you show them how.

The Value Of A "Spirited" Player

I wish I had a nickel for every time I saw an undisciplined team with players who threw temper tantrums, taunted other players, climbed on the fence, and performed other animal acts whose behavior and activities were rationalized by their coaches or parents who explained that a particular player's "spirited" manner was what made him a great player. Of course, I'm being generous in describing bad on-the-field behavior as "spirited" behavior. In my mind, silence is consent in this area and if the coach does not control player behavior on the field, he will soon have a group of selfish individuals rather than a team. These players bring the team down when they're down and they help the team shine when they shine. The problem is that

51

everyone makes errors and has bad games, so errors must be shaken off by players, coaches, and parents, regardless of their magnitude and effect on the score. Remember perspective... Unless players play as a team, one player's bad day will become a bad day for the whole team. They should be taught to redirect this energy  to become team leaders. Coaches need to concentrate their efforts toward accomplishing team goals, not toward coddling the undisciplined few.

I never threatened players, partly because it accentuates the negative, but also because a threat becomes an opportunity for a problem player to grandstand at the coach's expense. I made the rules early on and everyone knew what was going on. When a team rule was breached, we responded quickly and handled it without hoopla. I did not lecture the player in front of others before or after he ran his lap or was put on the bench. He did his thing then we moved on. I normally took some time later to privately ensure the player understood what the problem was. Problems were very, very rare once the pattern was set. This allowed us to concentrate on playing the game.

By the middle of my final season, our players were talking to each other about where the play was, they were telling their coaches what they would do on a pop fly before the coach had a chance to tell them, and they didn't need an adult in the dugout to keep the batting order and behavior in order because they did it themselves. I didn't make a big deal of it — we simply presumed this level of performance and behavior of them from the very beginning and we didn't flinch. It was a self-fulfilling expectation.

Watch Them Mimic

Players tend to imitate those they think are good at what they do. So do adults, for that matter, but kids do it shamelessly. Be aware of what they are seeing and when you see them imitate something that is inconsistent with good ball, step in. Remember that just because your players did it right for you today, there is no assurance that they will do it right tomorrow. Be persistent and don't be afraid to rehash old material.

Can Girls Play This Game?

My use of the words "he" and "him" throughout this book is not intended to imply that this is a boy's sport, because it's not. Without getting into a discussion of human development, let me just say that as far as I can tell, girls and boys in this age group are nearly uniformly capable of playing this game. Girls are like boys in that they will achieve largely according to the expectations placed upon them. If coaches or parents treat them like cute little girls acting like ballplayers, they will not be very valuable to the team. If you're the parent of a ballplayer, whether he is male or she is female, treat him or her like a ballplayer and he or she will play like one.

Chapter 5

THE FIRST TEAM MEETING

- Give Them A Newsletter
- Set The Ground Rules
- Solicit Questions
- Leave The Door Open
- Be Positive And Enthusiastic

As we've already seen, parents bring their own expectations into the season and it's safe to assume that coaches and managers do the same. The best way to ensure there are no surprises as the season develops is for the manager to hold a meeting and set the tone early. He should let the parents know that he knows what he's doing and help them develop confidence in him during this first team meeting.

Give Them A Newsletter

One of the first things a manager should do before practice begins is write a newsletter and give it to the parents. I was advised to do this my first season and it was some of the best advice I got. It gave me an opportunity to lay some essential groundwork for the parents and get the season off the ground. The morale of the parents on your team is DIRECTLY related to the extent to which their expectations are met. Unless you write them a newsletter, they will create their own expectations — chances are you will not meet them all. For my money, the following elements are essential parts of an effective newsletter:

Welcome

Send them a handshake on paper. Describe the season's routine and eliminate potential surprises. The parents of your players, like all of us, hate unnecessary surprises. You might be surprised to see how quickly a coach can be viewed as a "taker" rather than a "giver" when parents' expectations aren't fulfilled.

Practice frequency and duration

Again, let them know what to expect. Try to be at practice on time and ask them to do the same. Tell them that you're counting on their player to be there so you can build a team. Let them know that this is a team sport and that you can't build a team unless everyone shows up. Tell them that if their player can't make it, call so you can plan accordingly. If they don't call, call them to make sure everything's okay.

Unless you put commitment behind your policies, those policies will soon disappear. By the same token, try to end your practices on time. This is a subtle way to "meet them in the middle" on the promptness issue.

Give them a team roster and a phone list

A team roster helps parents become acquainted and helps foster a sense of "team" even among the parents. Parents often also work out car pools and such which tends to draw them closer as well.

Philosophy

Tell them right off the bat what your personal philosophy is. I told the parents of my players that my personal philosophy was that the development of our children was the point of youth athletics. I assured them that their children would become more mature mentally and physically as a result of their experience on the team and I added that the transition would be exciting to watch and participate in. I told them that this sport is about giving children a taste of competitive gamesmanship and developing basic baseball playing skills through hard work, encouragement, and the development of confidence, teamwork, and sportsmanship. I told them that if we were successful in this effort, the children would enjoy what they were doing. I added that, of course, we would formulate strategies and game plans and we'd talk to our players about winning because that's the point of competition. I added, however, that we would not win at all costs, nor would we miss the opportunity to teach our players how to be graceful losers when or if we lost games.

I set no expectations on winning — remember that winning often requires the unwilling participation of the opposition. While you can control your team's preparation, you cannot control the other team's preparation. Setting expectations for winning is a good way to make a successful season seem unsuccessful when or if you lose a couple of games along the way.

Set The Ground Rules

Rules about having players to practice on time, coaching the kids from the sideline, being supportive and positive fans, working with the kids at home, show time for games, bringing refreshments to the dugout during games (ask them not to do it) are examples of issues you should deal with early.

Let them know, for instance, that when parents coach from outside the fence, the effect is quite distracting to the team. Players need to recognize their coaches as their on-the-field authority.

Solicit Questions

Most parents don't know anything about this game and there will be a lot of things they will be left wondering about as time goes on. It is better for you that they bring their questions to you so you can give it to them from the horse's mouth.

Leave The Door Open

Invite their questions and comments as the season goes on, but set some ground rules. You do not need parents interrupting practices and games unless there's something that can't wait. Discussions with parents about their children can be quite lengthy and detailed; you really can't count on giving them a fair and adequate hearing if you're splitting your attention. This meeting with the parents might be important to the child and you need to make sure you give the parents your best insight. Keep in mind that Jimmy's parents are a bit biased in their view of their child when they do come up to you. Don't do anything about that — just be aware of it because a concerned parent isn't always an objective one. Listen intently to their concerns, but don't change the batting order every time a parent talks to you about their kid. You need to make decisions on the basis on what YOU believe is right. Decisions made out of expediency (to get the parents off of your back) will haunt you. Someone or your team will suffer because you didn't have the courage to make the "right" decision.

Be Positive And Enthusiastic

Be positive and enthusiastic: Parents have to *want* to turn their kids over to you on the ballfield. Unless they've been living in a vacuum, your parents will be wary of the influence you're going to have on their children. Consider their perspective and help them believe in what you're doing. Remember that you not only have to elicit a specific response from your players, you also have to get the parents on board with you, too. One of the biggest mistakes I've seen coaches make is being indifferent and incommunicative to the parents.

Chapter 6

PRACTICE

- The Basics
- Warm-Up
- Repetition
- Practice The Way You Want To Play
- Drills
- Bring Water
- Discipline
- Split-Squad Practices

If you practice or work with your child so infrequently that you can't see any skill development, you either need to stop practicing or practice more often. If you're practicing as much as you should, but you're still not seeing any development, you need to beef up your routine. The only way to build a good team out of a group of individuals is through effective practice. On the field, you have to be a teacher as well as a coach. Teach them what they need to know, show them what you taught them, practice the things you taught them over and over, then be prepared to do it all over again. The same applies to individual players in their personal development away from the team. Parents need to work with their children often and in a manner that helps them become more effective with their team.

The Basics

A lot of a child's playing success will depend on his ability to consistently apply basic skills; this fundamental concept is amplified when applied to a team. Emphasize these basics at home, at practice, and during games. Since the primary benefit of organized practice is to teach players to play and perform as a team, coaches gain the maximum benefit from their practices when players continue to work at home on the individual skills they learn at practice. Parents will benefit from listening to what their coaches are telling their children so they can further develop their skills at home. As we've already discussed, however, parents need draw the line when it comes to stepping in while they're being coached on the field.

With that said, coaches should not feel threatened about inviting parents to help warm the team up before practices and games; there might be times when coaches will want to ask for their help when they're shorthanded during practice and games.

Warm-Up

Before every practice and every game, spend some time warming up. As soon as two players arrive to begin warming up their arms, have them do so. Once the team's arms are warm, do some stretching and other warm-up exercises. Loosen the muscles in their arms and legs and get their heart rate up a little. As time goes on and you get a routine established, count on the players to lead the exercises (under your supervision).

Repetition

Practice, by definition, presumes repetition. If you don't repeat drills and skills, your players' development will tail off. By the same token, you have to practice often enough to make a difference. You will have to figure out how much is enough, but understand that if your players' progress perishes between practices, then you're doing something wrong. There is also such a thing as too much practice unless you innovate and give them something new to learn. You don't want them to get burned out by mid-season. My teams practiced four times a week before the games began, fewer times during the season.

Some might think that four times is excessive; other might think it's not enough. Here's how I look at it: I look at learning baseball the same way I look at learning to play the piano. There is no way a piano player can learn to make magic on the keyboard unless he's at it every day. We can probably agree on that because we all know there's a lot to learning to play the piano. The same is true of baseball; and anyone who thinks you can run out of things to teach a tee ball player in four practices a week probably doesn't understand the game.

Repetition is the keystone of successful game preparation. However, repetition soon turns to monotony with players, particularly tee ball players, unless you:

- PLAN every aspect of every practice right down to the minute. Lay your plan out on a clipboard with your watch nearby until you get comfortable with the timing and stick to it. Make copies of your plan and give them to your coaches or your parent helpers for the day and keep them to it. The best way to meet your season's goals is to meet daily goals.

- There should be a distinct sense of MOTION to your practices and a coherent FLOW to them. Tee ball players standing by idly are a problem. If you keep them in motion, you'll improve their conditioning and help them develop their mental awareness.

- Make a GAME out of as many things as you can. Try to have your players compete in teams as much as possible to get them used to winning, losing, and cooperating as a team. Remember, however, that the game is not more important than the skill you're trying to develop. The game that loses track of skill development is a waste of valuable time. Don't get so caught up in the game or in the drill that you don't take the time to correct errors. If you have a spare parent or coach, have him pull players who are having a particularly difficult time aside for more individual attention.

Practice The Way You Want To Play

The individual attention you can give to your players is also advantageous. You have to have specific objectives in mind when you meet to practice; otherwise, the investment of time and work will be wasted. Remember that players will not perform effectively in games unless they have practiced that way. If you don't practice base running, you will get base running outs in games. If you don't drill the players on catching the ball and making a good, smart throw, they won't do it in the game. Attention to the basics is essential. Teach players to look for the 3rd base coach when they're approaching 2nd base. Teach them how and when to slide. Drill them on base running scenarios. Drill them on defensive setups. There are dozens of things to do and not enough time to do it.

Drills

Drills are simply time-saving tools for focusing on and developing essential basic skills. They are critical to the proper development of your players and as I said in another part of this book, unless you deal with a skill or scenario in practice, you cannot expect your players to play the way you want them to during the game. The drills that follow are described with the coach in mind, but most can be performed at home as well.

I've talked to a number of coaches who have expressed frustration over their inability to improve their team at practice in spite of lengthening the sessions and practicing more often. In 99% of these cases, the coach's practice consisted of one practice "station" with a lot of kids standing around when he could have been working three stations with kids remaining in MOTION. The reason his practices weren't as productive as he wanted them to be was because his team only really practiced for 20 minutes of the hour he had them there. To make the most of your practice time, break the team up into two or three groups, depending on the number of coaches, space, and equipment you have available for the workout. This will enable you to accomplish two or three times as much work without making players stand around with nothing to do. This will also give you that element of MOTION and FLOW we discussed earlier.

Set goals for them. Divide the team into two teams and keep track of how they're doing in a "drill competition." On running and hitting drills, keep score — tell them how many runs it takes to win the game. On defensive drills, do likewise — keep score and clean the bases after three outs. This makes the practice more exciting and keeps the GAME element in there.

Chart skill development and give some recognition of players' achievement of milestones. Typically, this is best done on a one-to-one basis at this age — players are easily discouraged when they perceive they are being singled out as lagging behind the rest of the team. The focus of tee ball is on development, rather than on categorical assessments.

The Crab

This drill is intended to get players in the habit of moving in side-straddle strides to the ball when it's in range to do so. The players are lined up in front of a coach who holds a ball near the ground to simulate an oncoming ground ball. He moves the ball left and right and the players "crab" to the ball accordingly.

Throw To The Bucket

This drill is intended to get players in the habit of delivering low-trajectory balls to a target from long distance. The players are lined up in right field, then center field, then left field. An empty bucket is laid on its side just on the first base side of second base (for a tag throw). A coach stands in the outfield with a bucket of balls and drops them, one at a time, in front of players who, in turn, quickly pick the ball up and fire it to the bucket. It is better that the ball arrive on a bounce than have a high trajectory.

Back To The Bucket — Ball Against The Fence

As with the Throw To The Bucket drill, put a coach and the fielders in the outfield with a bucket of balls and an empty bucket at second base. This time, however, have the players face the outfield fence when the coach throws the ball against the fence. Teach players to field the dead ball bare-handed, turn in the direction of their glove hand (to the left for right-handed throwers), and fire the ball to the bucket at second base. (Be careful not to give the impression that we prefer to field balls hit to the outfield off of the fence or they will learn to run to the fence for every ball hit there!)

Throw Only

This drill is intended to get players in the habit of quickly delivering the ball to the target. Line the players up at third base. With a coach at first base, then at second base, position another coach at third base with a bucket of balls. The coach at third base drops the ball at the player's feet so the player can pick it up. Once the ball is touched by the player, the coach counts to three with the idea that the ball should be handled and thrown hard to first or second base before the count of three. This allows every player on the team to practice throwing balls fielded from the ground without having to fuss over bobbled balls along the way.

Double Play Ball

You won't turn them unless you practice them, and yes, tee ball players can "turn two." Line players up at the shortstop and second base positions with a coach and a bucket of balls in front of the second base bag and another at first base to take the throw. Randomly alternate between rolling grounders to shortstop and second base with the other player covering the bag and feeding the ball to first base. Set up scenarios where the player takes the play at second base himself.

Dish And Darts

How many times have you seen an easy infield put-out ruined because the fielder standing only a few feet away threw the ball too hard or lobbed it and left it hanging in the air? The Dish and Darts drill is designed to give players work in making the right kind of throw in the right situation.

When you're looking for a quick feed when the players are too close to each other to haul off and throw it (the distance varies for tee ball players), have them practice "dishing" the ball to the baseman with an underhand toss fed with a flat trajectory. This is accomplished by leaning forward at the waist and stepping into the toss with the non-throwing foot as in throwing horseshoes. The dish is useful when feeding a double-play ball to second base.

When you're looking for a relatively short throw when you have a little more time to make it, have them practice the "dart" throw. This is particularly useful for balls hit to the pitcher for a play at first base. The player should take a few quick steps toward the bag as he brings the ball up in front of his shoulder, forward of his head. From there, he tosses the ball as if throwing a dart. This toss puts the ball up where the first baseman can see it coming and is generally very accurately delivered.

Field Only

Players can be lined up in two or three different positions on the infield from which they will each field balls hit by a coach. Once they field a ball, they quickly roll it to the side and prepare to field another. This allows every player on the team to field dozens of balls in a very short time.

Base Running Situations

This drill is good for the last item of the day. Line players up at home plate with the first base coach at first base and the third base coach at third base. Have them simulate a swing of the bat (with no bat) and run down to first base. Practice various scenarios; again, they won't get it unless you practice it. This drill is so important that I have dedicated entire practices to base running only. There are more details on base running later in this book.

Hitting And Running

Practice the batting order. Get them used to hitting, DROPPING the bat, and running to first base. It's important to get them up there to get repetitions with the bat, but it is also important to get them to go "live" so they have an eye for how it all comes together. If, during your first real game, one of your players runs to third base instead of first base, you'll wish you'd run this drill. This is a drill that would never occur to you to run until after the first error is made. It seems not to occur to us adults that someone could run to third base instead of first.

Before Game/After Game Routine

The best way to get your players used to the pre-game and post-game routine is to use it for practice. Before every practice we warmed up our arms and did some exercises.

After that we huddled, where I discussed our goals for the day and recapped our success to date. After a few other words, we broke out of the huddle. We had a similar routine after the practice, except that I always reminded them that I was proud of how hard they were working. Aside from the game context, the pre- and post-game routines were very much the same as the practice routine.

Dugout Behavior

Proper dugout behavior is essential to good order on the ballfield during the game. As with all of these drills, if you don't achieve it in practice, you won't achieve it in the game. A dugout full of monkeys is very distracting to the team and the coaches. It also sets the tone for what will happen between the baselines.

Glove Reaction Drill

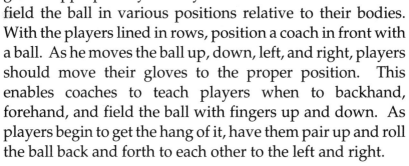

This drill is intended to get players to position their gloves appropriately as they field the ball in various positions relative to their bodies. With the players lined in rows, position a coach in front with a ball. As he moves the ball up, down, left, and right, players should move their gloves to the proper position. This enables coaches to teach players when to backhand, forehand, and field the ball with fingers up and down. As players begin to get the hang of it, have them pair up and roll the ball back and forth to each other to the left and right.

Hitting Between The Buckets

When I practiced the batting order, I put red plastic buckets in the field where the defense would be set. We created offensive scenarios with our batters and told them to drive the ball in a gap, normally chosen by the batting coach. If the ball was hit too softly or too closely to a bucket, we counted the hit as an out. This kept them from depending on a player to make an error for them to get on base.

Hitting Stations

Cut lengths of 1" to 1-1/2" PVC pipe for each member of the team and ask parents to tape the "handle" of the pipe bat for their player. Make the PVC bat part of their equipment that they bring to games and practices. Make or find yourself a backstop and set up two stations hitting off of the tee and a third station working on the fundamentals of the swing. With a team of twelve players, you can keep three groups of four actively engaged in the art of hitting — again, the key is repetitions. Your investment here will help them immensely in later years.

• Station #1 — Under the close supervision of a coach who recognizes the fundamentals of an effective swing, work with players on every aspect, both in stop motion and full speed with their PVC bats.

• Station #2 — Set up a tee with whiffle ball baseballs that they hit with their PVC bats into a backstop. This will improve their hand-eye coordination and force them to hit the ball with the sweet spot of the bat. Vary the station by using plastic golf balls on occasion.

• Station #3 — Set up a tee with regular Tee Ball baseballs that they hit with a Tee Ball bat into a backstop (it can be the other side of the Station #2 backstop). Practice full, powerful swings, focusing on the fundamentals. Vary batter positions in the batter's box in order to develop place hitting and "knob drive" covered later in this book. I recommend that you cut mats out of indoor/outdoor carpeting or some other material in the dimensions of a regulation batter's box for hitting drills. They are portable and indispensable aids in practice.

Pop Flies

You should operate a pop fly station at every practice. Teaching them to catch pop flies is covered in more detail later in this book, but you need to drill the techniques you've taught them. Get them to run to the ball first, keeping an eye on it as he goes, THEN catch it. Keep it simple at first, then make the routine more challenging. It is very important to teach your players about cutting off the ball angle. Draw it out for them in the dirt. If you don't teach this, they will do what I mentioned in the Back To The Bucket drill and simply run to the fence on outfield balls.

Race The Ball

You want your players to learn NOT to chase balls but to track them down by anticipating where the path of the ball will intersect the path they take in getting to it. Make a game of cutting the ball off by racing the ball to a point. The key is to ultimately get your players to arrive at that point just before the ball does. Vary the exercise by having them come up throwing to a base.

Hustle

Although there is not a "Hustle" drill, you need to have your players hustle all of the time: hustle on and off of the field, hustle from station to station, hustle to and from huddles, and hustle on all plays (even when they don't have a chance to even touch the ball).

Save The Best For Last

Learn what your players' favorite drill is in the batch that you're using on a given day and save it for near the end of practice. This develops in them the sense that practice and tee ball is fun throughout, even when it's work. Once in a while, have parents surprise them with pizza and drinks after a practice AT the practice field.

Bring Water

Have the players' parents bring personal water bottles for their kids for practices and games. If they do not drink water, especially when it's hot, they might dehydrate and become ill. At a minimum, their performance and concentration will go right down the tubes.

Discipline

It's only a matter of time before you have to discipline a player for being disruptive or some other breach of teamwork. While taking a lap is good for mental mistakes to promote concentration, laps don't work well for violations of team rules at practice. I had players sit off to the side for a few minutes while we continued with practice. This accomplished two things: First, it showed them that the team could still function without them. Second, it made them realize how much they like being part of the action. When you keep practice in MOTION, players want to be a meaningful part of it.

Split-Squad Practices

Don't be afraid to split your team into smaller sessions when you want to focus on one aspect of practice, such as hitting. By splitting the squad, you can get even more direct work because you're working with a smaller group of players at a time. You can continue to work stations, but you can do it with a two players per station rather than four. Arrange a switch-over time when the other half of the team arrives and the first half leaves. It is VERY important that parents meet practice times for split-squad sessions so you can stay on track.

A variation on the split-squad practice are sessions you have with select groups: infielders, outfielders, or players having trouble with certain fundamentals, and so forth.

Chapter 7

OFFENSE

- Hitting Basics
- Hitting For Results
- Base Running
- Offensive Strategy

You hear about "natural hitters," but I don't think I've ever met one. I've run into a lot of players who worked hard to develop their skills, but none that were just born with "it." Their hard work produced dividends for them and won them admiring observers who just knew they were looking at "natural hitters." Here are some tips for getting some of those "natural hitters" on your team.

Hitting Basics

In Tee Ball, the coach positions his hitters in the batter's box so they can properly address the ball on the tee. Proper positioning of the hitter is not only essential to the development of solid hitting skills, it is also the key element in offensive strategy. The coach is well-advised to spend a lot of time working with his players in the batter's box in various situations. Players need to learn to follow directions in the batter's box so they can learn place-hitting and coaches need to learn the relationship between batter's positioning and ball placement while sticking to the hitting fundamentals that will serve the players as they advance in the baseball ranks.

The Batting Stance

Unfortunately, relatively few Tee Ball players are taught the fundamental elements of hitting and many others are forced into uncomfortable or ineffective hitting stances and strides, or both. The result is that many players move on with poorly developed baseball hitting skills, and have trouble adapting as they go.

There is plenty of room for personal creativity with regard to the stance as long as some key considerations are preserved. First of all, the feet are best positioned at least shoulder's width apart, toes toward the plate with the hitter's head erect. In other words, the eyes should be fairly parallel to the ground with both eyes focused on the ball. Players who stand with their feet too close together tend to over-stride and swing off-balance. Those who have their feet too far apart tend to have a problem transferring their weight and power during the swing.

As you're working with your tee ball players, try to avoid letting hitters stand nearly motionless in one position in the batter's box too long. When a batter stands in one place too long, he tends to settle vertically in his stance while he's waiting to swing. This makes it difficult for him to transfer this momentum horizontally into his hitting motion. Unfortunately, this is difficult to prevent in Tee Ball because, appropriately, Tee Ball Baseball rules normally allow the hitter only one practice swing and the batter is not permitted to shuffle his feet once the ball is placed on the tee. Once the coach puts the hitter in the box, the umpire should move promptly to place the ball on the tee. This promptness keeps the game moving and keeps the hitter in motion.

The Stride

Whatever the coach does with foot positioning during the hitting sequence, he must ensure the batter maintains control over his power and balance and can reach the ball with the "sweet" part of the bat. As the stride is begun with the batter's weight and head back over the back foot and weight on the balls of the feet, the batter transfers his weight in the swing with the head kept back behind the point of contact with the ball.

The hitter is allowed reasonable latitude with regard to hand and bat position in his initial stance as he waits to drive the ball. However, it is essential that during the first part of the actual swing, the front elbow is kept down and bent at a 90 degree angle with the bat handle further from the pitcher than the bat barrel. In other words, with the front elbow down, ensure the hitter's top hand is closer to the pitcher than the bottom hand and the wrists are not cocked. I tried to keep my hitters' hands positioned in front of their back shoulder because it seemed to be the best position from which to initiate a level swing. Hands that are begun either much higher or much lower than that can easily travel an inconsistent route to the point of contact, resulting in an equally inconsistent contact and flight of the ball.

The function of the stride is often overlooked. It is useful as a way to help overcome that vertical momentum discussed already and the length of the stride also plays a role in place-hitting in Tee Ball. The length of the stride varies between hitters and situations, but should never be exaggerated to the extent that the player's weight is ineffectively distributed. For many hitters and in many situations, the player might need to set up already in some degree of a stride then simply pick his foot up and put it down as he transfers power in the swing.

Knob Drive

READ THIS VERY CAREFULLY: The very end of the handle of the bat is the "knob." The hitter needs to be perfectly tuned into how he drives the knob of his bat in his swing. The knob of the bat needs to be driven away from the body for hits to the opposite field and more toward the body for "pulled" hits (thus, the term "pull hitter"). Too many coaches and parents emphasize the sense of "swing" in teaching hitters what to do with the bat when instead, they should be drilling the idea of "driving" the knob through ball contact, thus "driving" the bat head through the ball and "driving" the ball off the tee into the field of play.

A properly driven knob will prevent the hitter from prematurely extending his back arm prior to ball contact. Full extension of that arm should not occur until just after ball contact. Early extension of that arm results in a dipping of the bat head in a roundhouse approach to the ball, resulting in the "tee ball home run swing." I call it the "tee ball home run swing" because tee ball is the only baseball game where the hitter will ever get away with a swing like that. In baseball, he becomes a strikeout victim because he can't get the bat head to the ball in time with that route of travel. Even when he does get there in time, the travel of the bat has a vertical component that means that his swing has to be perfectly timed to hit the center of the ball. The knob-driven swing places the travel of the bat head in the same plane as the travel of the typical incoming fast ball. Even with pitched balls that "move around," the knob-driven swing is efficient enough to put the bat on the ball quickly and is perfect for "protecting the plate" with two strikes.

The Back Foot

In baseball, with the hitter's weight transferred from over the back foot, the direction of the batted ball's travel depends upon the inside/outside location of the ball relative to the plate when it's hit and the ahead/further ahead location of the ball relative to the back foot when ball contact is made. We'll go into this a little more in the next section on place hitting, but let's cast a vote now for the importance of that back foot.

During the swing, that back foot plays a tremendous role in the flight of the ball with regard to POWER. Weight is transferred from over the back foot in coordination with a rotation of the foot about the ball of the foot and a rotation of the hips and shoulders. However, the hitter's weight should not be transferred forward of where contact is made with the ball.

Try this: Stand up and go through a swinging motion (knob drive) without rotating your back foot, hips, and shoulders. Now you know just how important these rotations are.

Now, go to the other extreme: In advance of your knob drive, go through a full rotation of your back foot, hips, and shoulders. You can almost feel your power dissipate in advance of your swing.

Somewhere between the two extremes is where you want to

be. The back foot, hips, and shoulders should rotate in coordination with the knob drive in a manner that your power is transferred, through the bat to the ball at the point of impact. Errors in coordination toward either of the two extremes results in an early or late transferral of power. The laces of that back shoe should be pointed in roughly the same direction as the intended flight of the ball.

It is very important that hitters not "throw" their hips or transfer their weight ahead of the bat swing. All of this body motion needs to be coordinated in a manner that gives the bat "pop" at the point of contact with the ball.

I think it is better to describe what players do with the bat as "slinging" it through the strike zone rather than "swinging" it. To me, slinging it implies some snap at some point. It requires the hitter to drive the bat head to the ball. Swinging it opens a range of possibilities. The hands should travel across and close to the body, not out and away from it through the swing. Watch your batter's back elbow. If it straightens early in the swing, he is not driving his hands through the strike zone and is probably dipping the bat head en route to the ball. Dipping the bat head results in pop flies and mis-hit balls.

Stand up again and take another adult by the shoulders with your feet in a batting position. Now, through a coordination of back foot, hip, and shoulder rotation move that adult by his shoulders as if in a swing follow-through. Unless you drive off of your back foot — or to put it another way, grind your back foot into the ground — you will not displace that adult as much as you are physically capable.

Watch that back foot and see where the weight is placed. The weight should be placed on the insteps of both feet. Chances are that if the hitter has his weight on the outside of his back foot through ball contact, he probably also dipped his bat and did not drive the knob.

Hands At The Point Of Ball Contact

It is essential to develop in your players the habit of keeping the barrel of the bat above the hands during the swing all the way to the ball.   As we've already discussed, some coaches allow their hitters to drop the bat barrel so they can launch the ball deep into the outfield, and we now know that's bad for your hitters.   Get power with good fundamentals and by ensuring your hitter's hands are palm-up and palm-down at the point of ball contact, not by sweeping wide and up with the bat.

Hitting For Results

Place Hitting

Place hitting is the only way to reliably defeat the advantage a skilled defense has over the hitter. Most coaches limit their ball placement efforts to varying the batter's position in the batter's box. However, in the paragraphs that follow, I will describe a dimension of hitting that can really liven up the game and give player skill and bat and body control a larger

role in the game while applying many of the principles discussed in the previous paragraphs.

The coach who positions the batters in the batter's box must have some sense of where he wants his batter to hit the ball. He must keep in mind that the opposing coaches are watching his eyes and his batter's eyes to gain some hint of their plans. A good hitter does not tip his hand to the other team so they can gain the advantage over him. (This is why our players didn't take practice swings when they stepped into the box.) In placing the Tee Ball hitter in the box, there are four factors that play a huge role in where the ball will go when it is hit. The first is the batter's position in the batter's box, the second is the extent to which weight is transferred forward during the batter's stride, the third is the position of the batter's hands as the swing develops (knob drive), and the fourth is foot, hip, and shoulder rotation. (For simplicity's sake this discussion will take the right handed batter's perspective. All the rules apply to the other side of the plate as well.)

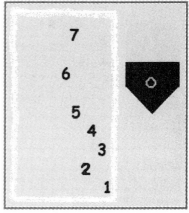

As a rule, if you want the hitter to hit to the left side he needs to stand deep in the box. For example, referring to the diagram of the batter's box and tee, the best place to position the back foot for a hit down the 3rd base line is in position 1. If the batter's back foot is positioned more toward position 2 or 3, the ball will be hit toward the shortstop. With the back foot near position 4, the ball can be placed in the middle of the field. A back foot placed near position 5 will make the ball move just to the right of 2nd base, and if placed near position 6 the ball will come closer to going down the right field line. The coach should take care to avoid going much further forward of position 6 with the rear foot because the batter will be more likely to step out of the batter's box from that position. Some coaches put the batter's back foot near position 7 and essentially turn the batter's back to the field as he attempts to have the batter hit the ball to right field. Don't do this. This is another one of those things that is not good for anything other than the game of tee ball. Remember that we're trying to develop baseball players, not career tee ball players.

Since the Tee Ball is not pitched to the batter, the batter is left to hit the ball from where he stands without place hitting the ball with an early or late swing and without "going with" the inside or outside pitch. With this understood, many Tee Ball coaches use a compact stride (small step with the lead foot) to help the batter pull the ball and a longer stride to help the batter push the ball to the opposite field. Again, referring to the diagram above, notice that with a more compact stride with the back foot in position 1, the batter is more likely to hit the ball down the 3rd base line. However, if the batter "steps

In the bucket

in the bucket" with the lead foot toward position 2, he will probably "cue stick" the ball (nub the ball off the end of the bat) with marginal results. The more he strides and transfers weight toward position 3 or 4, the more his power dissipates and the ball moves toward the middle. This movement of the ball toward the middle can create the opportunity to have the batter place hit the ball from one batting stance with nearly 90 degrees of range, but teaching him to over-stride is not good for the batter. Therefore, if you're using the stride to alter the direction of the flight of the ball, make sure you haven't produced a hitting position that will be useless to him later. (Incidentally, when planning a defense, it's worthwhile to notice the strides of opposing players. This will help you predict the power and direction of the ball's travel.)

The hitter should begin his stride to get the swing started then coordinate the rotation and knob drive. Remember the role of the rotation of the back foot, hips, and shoulders. It's easy to see why the opposite field hit tends to be weaker — not as much hip rotation to get the ball to the opposite field. If the coach wants the batter to nail the 3rd base line, he should have the batter rotate those hips hard. However, if you mention "hips" to a tee ball player he will give you that "deer-in-the-headlights" stare. Refer to his belly button and he will relate instantly. If you tell the tee ball player to aim his belly button and shoe laces toward the hole he's hitting to, he will have the best opportunity to swing with maximum power. Again, in tee ball player terminology, when I wanted to get the hands where I wanted them, I told the batter to point his front elbow (while keeping it down) toward the hole he was hitting to at the point of contact between the bat and the ball. This will help you get the knob driven where you want it.

Pop Flies

If you've spent any time around Tee Ball at all, you've seen coaches who framed their entire offensive strategy around a scheme to have hitters challenge the outfield's ability to catch the ball by hitting pop flies. However, when the level of competition elevates, those deep fly balls turn into disappointing outs. My teams scored a lot of runs just by hitting hard grounders and crisp line drives through holes in the defense.

Line Drives And Grounders

As you might gather, since I virtually eliminated the pop fly from my offensive scheme, I relied heavily on sharp line drives and grounders. When I say line drives I am talking about balls that seldom are as high as the ball player's head. The grounders are not dribblers that roll off the top of the tee; these balls are driven from the tee and not merely hit. A friend of mine who coached another team called them worm burners; we called them ankle cutters. You get the idea. A lot of coaches raise the tee too high, often shoulder-high. I almost always adjusted the tee to its lowest position to make it easier for the hitter to make good contact in a typical strike zone.

Gappers

Some coaches had the same attitude about hitting grounders and line drives as they had about hitting fly balls: they hit them blindly, hoping and assuming that the play would not be made by the defense. I always assumed the opposite. We were not satisfied when our hitters made it to the base on the basis of a fielder's error. We intended the first resort to be to hit away from the fielder or to his non-glove hand. The second resort was to count on the sharply hit ball being too difficult to field cleanly. Remember that a line drive hit right to the fielder is no different than the ball he caught when he warmed up before the game — it's easy to catch.

Base Running

Sliding Situations

Teach your players how to slide. Sliding is not only a safer way to go into a base when someone is already there, it also improves the runner's chance of being safe on the play. Obviously, you don't want them to slide on every play. You don't want them to slide at first base, for instance, and I would strongly discourage having them slide at home plate because of the tee. If the runner is at first base and the next hitter hits a line drive in the gap in the outfield, you don't want him to slide at second base while the coach is giving him the "come on" sign at third base. However, you might want him to slide at third base when he gets there. We coached our runners to slide at second base on any infield hit.

How To Slide

There are several sliding techniques you can teach your players, but I found that the basic bent-leg slide is more than suitable for most Tee Ball situations. Of course, you'll always see those players who want to be like Pete Rose and do a head-first slide, but you shouldn't let them do it at this age. The average tee ball player should begin the bent-leg slide about five feet from the bag, keeping in mind that distance is an individual thing that depends on player size and speed. You don't want him to slide so closely to the bag that he hits the bag hard; nor do you want him to start so far away that he doesn't make it to the bag at all. The idea here is for the player to launch himself (without bounding up into the air) then tuck that launching leg underneath himself. As the runner hits the dirt, he should sit back and ride it out with the other leg extended and slightly bent to prevent jamming the knee. It is important to practice sliding so players do it effectively, but it's also important to practice it so your players lose their sense of falling during the slide. The slide should carry the heel of the lead foot across the top of the bag so the runner doesn't crash into the bag. Runners should be ready to continue play as appropriate, but make sure they stay with the bag until they receive other instructions or until they know where the ball is. Another benefit of the slide is that it helps prevent the runner from overrunning the bag.

1st Base Options

The first base coach has a series of base running options to choose from. The key to issuing good instructions is to know what the player needs to do and to speak and signal clearly, loudly, and concisely. On our team, these first base options were: "run through," "make a turn," and "go." When we told him to run through, we intended for him to tail into foul territory a short distance after crossing the bag. When we told him to make a turn, we intended for him to touch the inside part of the bag, push off and stop two steps toward second base, find the ball, and listen to the coach. When we told him to go, we intended for him to touch the inside part of the bag push off and sprint to second base, picking up his third base coach as he approached the bag.

Running On Balls Hit Through The Infield

When the ball was hit safely through the infield, we typically sent the runner at first base on to third base unless we suspected the play would be made at third base. We nearly always sent him to third base if the ball was hit safely into right field.

Watching For The 3rd Base Coach

As the runner approaches second base he should pick up (look at) the third base coach without slowing down. The third base coach has his work cut out for him as he becomes accustomed to giving  instructions to runners headed to home plate in time to pick up the runner at second base. Seldom is there ever a successful play made at home plate, but I wouldn't count on it.

Sending Him Home

If there was a decent chance for the runner to make it to home plate without being chased down, we sent him home so we could tend to the other runners. The other runners are more likely to be the objects of plays at their bases.

Two Steps On A Fly Ball

One of the most aggravating things to witness is a runner being "doubled up" because he ran on a fly ball. We coached our runners to take two steps on all fly balls until the ball was caught. If it was caught, we had them get right back to the base because official Tee Ball Baseball rules prevent them from advancing on a caught fly ball. The reason we had them take two steps off the bag is because official Tee Ball Baseball rules allow runners to advance to the next base as long as they're between bases by the time the ball is controlled by the fielder. Local rules might vary from place to place that affect this coaching decision, but the coaching principle remains the same.

A Runner At 2nd Base With Less Than Two Outs

With a runner at second base with less than two outs with a ball hit to the shortstop, we coached our players to take two steps off the bag and watch to see where the ball was thrown. If the shortstop threw the ball to first base, he ran; if not, our runner made the shortstop make a play on him to force him back to second base, allowing the hitter to arrive at first base safely. Again, the official rule about advancing runners once the fielder has control of the ball is the main consideration.

Offensive Strategy

The normal strategy is to have the first couple of batters hit the ball down the left side to force the long throw to first base. With runners at first and second, the coach needs to figure out a way to get his batter on first base without losing a runner in scoring position. Hitting holes in the defense is always the best way to go. Hitting holes behind runners is also good.

You can incorporate the place-hitting component of your game at any point. It works best when the other team stacks the defense to cover what your player appears to be planning by virtue of his placement in the batter's box. Place-hitting also helps when the third baseman is cheating heavily to cover the base line and leaves a gap toward the shortstop's non-glove side. Hitting to the non-glove side makes the hole bigger than it appears.

I tended to have a consistent-hitting, fast player bat first. Once he got on first base, I tended to have the next hitter hit the ball down the third base line or in the gap between shortstop and third base. The first batter generally beat the throw to second base. The third batter was a hitter who could spray the ball around the field from one location in the batter's box. The cleanup hitter hit the ball sharply and consistently, often ending up with a double. The fifth batter was usually a consistent hitter and fast, and the sixth batter was good at place-hitting and could hit behind the runner at first base.

The players are funny in the way they get into the offense. They'll often look one way and hit the ball somewhere else. They'll be very subtle about their movements around the bases, hoping they'll not be noticed by the defense. As I've said before, these skills are not developed unless you practice them, but I must emphasize that your players will not develop a sense of gamesmanship unless you first, teach them the ins and outs of the game and second, release them to innovate and create within the constraints of the general game scheme.

Bat Selection

Your player's parents just bought him a new bat. It is a legal Tee Ball bat in all respects, but he can't seem to get it around in the swing. As much time as you spend with him trying to get him to put some snap into his swing and keep the bat barrel above the hands, he can't quite do it because his bat is 2 or 3 ounces too heavy for him. This is a very common scenario and one that can be a source of anguish for parents who don't understand how to find the right bat for their child. As we've discussed, the bat should be the heaviest bat the player can handle in a fundamentally sound swing. The heavier bat gives the ball more punch as long as the hitter can effectively get it to the ball. However, the heaviest bat in town is no good in the hands of the player who can't effectively deliver it to the ball.

There are a lot of ways a coach can lose control of his team in a game, and a lot of it is, as I have said in previous pages, because he didn't develop a game plan that was reflective of the skills and habits he developed in practice. One of the most common, yet subtle hazards to the game plan as well as to the players involves the handling of bats by the players. I always kept the bats we were going to use in the game near me on a rack hung on the backstop. There were normally no more than five bats on the rack and it was our team policy that players didn't handle a bat unless a coach handed it to him.

It was funny sometimes to watch our players ready to bat with a bat at their feet, refusing to pick it up. However, it was also comforting to know that I didn't have to worry about kids being hit in the head by swinging bats or about players using bats they couldn't swing. You only have to witness one close call with a bat to understand the need for this policy.

Chapter 8

DEFENSE

- Catching
- Throwing
- Defensive Strategy

As unusual as this might sound, my team and the all star team during my third season really enjoyed playing defense. I'll admit that they liked hitting better, but they also loved having the opportunity to make great plays. They did make some great plays, too. Despite playing at an age where they were stereotyped against making the defensive plays, they routinely retired the other team quickly so they could bat again. As you could tell from the amount of print I dedicated to drills earlier in this handbook, practice is the key to success on defense. Practicing the right thing is how you will change a lucky catch into a routine play.

Catching

Fly Balls

The most common mistake parents make when they're teaching their kids to catch is that they don't make sure they get to the ball before they try to catch it. We taught our kids to catch pop flies in two steps: run and center up under the ball, then put your glove up and catch the ball. We taught them to catch the ball out in front of them at about eye level as much as possible. Once they get the hang of moving confidently to the ball and putting the glove up, complicate the play a little in practice and teach them about cutting off the angle and catching the ball on the run. In all cases, however, it is essential that they develop the habit of moving immediately to where they think the ball will fall. Don't allow them to drift toward the arc, make them run to the ball's destination. We always had our players call any fly ball they intended to catch.

Grounders

You can use your drills to get players to move properly to the ball. Once there, body, glove, and head positioning is essential. The player's posture should

channel the ball up into his body if it's not caught. The player should play every ball he can between his feet and out in front of his body. He should keep his rear end down almost squatting without actually sitting and keep his head down on the ball, watching it all the way into the glove. The button on top of his cap should be pointed in the direction from which the ball came. He should position his non-glove hand so it can follow the ball into the glove. This helps keep the ball in the glove and puts the player in a better position to come up and make a throw.

Diving Catches

You can tell when your players are getting their confidence on defense when they start making diving catches. Again, once one player successfully makes a 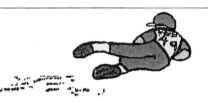 diving play, the others are soon to follow. The only problem is that you want to keep them on their feet unless there is no other way to make the play. Tee ball players love getting in the dirt on plays.

My brother had a routine with his kids that I copied and encouraged the parents of my players to adopt. He had an indoor-safe ball that he threw to them in their family room where they could get comfortable catching flies, grounders, and the really tough ones. They soon graduated to the really tough play made from the dive then they threw from the knees. This exercise is good for developing confidence around the ball and the repetitions it takes to become fluid in the fielding-throwing sequence. In my family, my boys and I played this game before they went to bed.

Throwing

The throw should be begun with the thrower squared to his target before swinging the throwing arm back with the upper body turning away with the arm, then finally rotating back toward the target with the throw. The player's eyes need to be kept on the target throughout with his shoulders kept level and his elbow leading the throw. As the arm travels rearward to begin the throw, the wrist and elbow should be rotated to put the ball to the rear (with the hand and wrist under the ball) at the furthest rearward travel of the ball. Once the arm begins its forward motion the hand and elbow are rotated again to put the ball to the front with the hand on top of the ball. The arm needs to stay up until the ball is released. The advancing foot needs to be planted in line with the direction of the throw while the player pushes off with the back foot. Tee ball players tend to throw with arm motions resembling catapults — this is called "pushing the ball." They need to put snap into their wrists as they release the ball, following through with the arm traveling across the body. It is essential that the player follow through with the arm and with the trailing leg stepping through. Tee ball players tend to snap their arms shortly after release without following through. The motion of the arm should be comparable to what you would imagine the motion of an elephant's trunk if it was throwing a ball — very fluid and smooth. Many young players become so concerned with accurate throws that they never learn to throw hard. If you can get them to cut loose with a hard throw, they will become disciplined in their accuracy over time.

Throwing From The Knees

You can develop a player's
throwing arm by drilling him
to throw from his knees. This is
one of those variations to your
practice that will keep your
players interested in ball.
Encourage your players to try the
throw from the knees in practice
and games if they have to,
provided they can make the
throw on a straight line. Kids take a long time
to get to their feet from their knees and they can make a lot
of things happen from the knees.

Defensive Strategy

A coach can learn a lot about defensive strategy and player placement by developing a coherent and effective offensive scheme. The principles are the same for everyone — the difference is the ability of the team to execute the scheme in question. It is very important for your hitters to understand what you're doing with them when they're batting because it will make it easier for them to read batters when they're on defense. I found the greatest success in positioning the Rover where I thought the ball would go then have the others close the lanes (gaps) to the fence.

Keep in mind that when fielders play in close, they have a smaller field to cover. However, they also have less time to react to what is happening on that field. You have to find the balance. I always had the outfielders (except for the Rover(s)) play two steps in front of the fence. This cuts down on a lot of running to the fence for balls that got by them.

Sometimes, I moved the outfield in close and at other times I played with two Rovers. Realize that any time you move an outfielder up you are risking extra base hits to the fence. You should only play with two Rovers if the second Rover can actually catch the ball. Two ball-catching Rovers sure shrink the playing field.

I generally had our players make all throws to second base from the outfield. However, if we were playing an aggressive base running team, we threw to third base once in a while to keep them honest. The key to slowing down an aggressive base running team is to make good throws from the outfield and catches at the bases. Your basemen have to know when to tag the runner and when to tag the base. Once you teach them when, you have to teach them how, then drill it.

During those seasons when I was short of players who could consistently make good plays, I made sure my second baseman was good enough to handle the force play at second base in case the runner made it to first. We stopped a lot of momentum at second base with that arrangement. When I had a solid team, that development of the play to second base became the first half of several double plays.

Make sure your players are always paying attention. As I have already said, you cannot expect your players to handle the game situation unless you have practiced it. Although we had our share of 4, 5, and 6 year old players, most of our players paid good attention most of the time because we made them understand that the next ball might be their opportunity to make the big play.

I seldom told the players where a particular play was supposed to go during the game — I asked them. In the past, I did tell them, but many was the time that I scratched my head wondering how they could stand there, hear me tell them where the play was going, then throw the ball somewhere else. I don't think they ever were not prepared when they told me where the ball was going.

It is very tough for tee ball players to get three outs on the other team. In 19 games during my third season, they got three outs in all but two innings that season. The players identify closely with your expectations of them. During that third season, our goal was to get three outs on the other team every inning. During our defensive drills in practice, we worked in cycles of three outs. Soon they identified with 3-out innings when they were on defense in games.

When the opposing offense does not place-hit, you can allow your players to "cheat" to narrow gaps where they think the ball will go. However, when you're playing teams that spray the ball around, you need your players to cover their positions fairly straight up. Your players can vary the look by shifting to a gap late and so on, but be very careful about presenting a look that becomes predictable and easy to beat.

During the regular season, we were allowed to place a coach outside the outfield fence to help the players know where to shift. However, we seldom did. Instead, we counted on our players to move to fill gaps with the exception of the Rover who I directed from the sideline. I held up a number of fingers that corresponded to an area of the field I wanted him to run to (1st base, 2nd base, 3rd base) and I shifted him from there. Once he was in the right area he was free to free-lance a bit to cover anything he saw from his vantage point. This was especially helpful during the Tee Ball World Series when we were not allowed to post a coach outside the fence. The nonverbal signals were also valuable during those games when the fans and other coaches are cheering and giving instructions.

Chapter 9

ONE MORE THING...

- The Umpires
- The Last Word...

While there is no assurance that your players will grow up to become professional baseball players, coaches can have a powerful influence on them as they enter what is likely their first encounter with organized athletics. Many professional baseball players got their start by playing Tee Ball for coaches like those coaching our children today. Coaching Tee Ball well is hard work, but it's work that pays great dividends to players as they continue to grow and to us as we look back fondly some day on the "good old days" when we coached them.

The Umpires

There are many perspectives in dealing with umpires, but here is mine. Rule #1 for dealing effectively with umpires: put yourself in their position. All things being equal, as long as the umpire is putting his best effort forward and has not made a call contrary to rules, most of what you have to say argumentatively will not be received very favorably. Some people believe that "the squeaky wheel gets the grease." In other words, the umpire doesn't really know that you expect a good call unless you let him know when he makes a bad one. Personally, as a coach I tried to be wary of showing umpires up or making them look bad, regardless of how bad I thought the call was. That doesn't mean we didn't discuss the bad calls or that he didn't get the opportunity to witness my looks of disbelief, but I did not get in the umpire's face or mutter under my breath during these Tee Ball games. Remember that judgment calls are not debatable, regardless of how gross the judgment might be.

One thing to watch for is some umpires' tendency to interject themselves too much into the outcome of the game. Their responsibilities are very specific and do not include balancing the score or amending the rules during the game. During my first season, we lost a lot of one-sided games and occasionally an umpire would make a call that went in our favor when it clearly should have gone against us. My opinion was, and still is, that there are always two sides of the coin. At the same time that the game became unrecoverable and the umpire felt compelled to even things out, the other manager had already made substitutions to help us match up a little more evenly and give his younger players a chance to play key positions. When the umpire calls my player safe after the other team's substitute made a great play to get him out, I believed a disservice is brought upon both players. My player needed to see what it was like to make an out when both players made a good play and the other team's player needed to experience the thrill of making a great play in a key position. I believe that one of the reasons my players matured so well was because we never threw in the towel or let them stop playing hard, even in those lopsided games. In this situation, the umpire became too aware of the score and essentially defeated objectives that both managers had for their teams. This is not normally a big problem and you can usually handle it quickly and quietly. Remember that the umpire is just trying to do the decent thing and is normally more than happy to stick to handling only the issues that call upon his objectivity and leave the balancing of the game to the managers and players.

The Last Word...

I have attempted to give you the answers to questions I didn't even know I had as I was trying to figure this game out. Managing and coaching is a tremendous challenge for anyone, particularly for that parent who's just trying to make sure his child has a decent person for a coach. Parenting a young tee ball player is also difficult when all you want for your child is for him to enjoy himself and learn cooperative and athletic skills.

In this book, I've discussed the building of the team and coaching staff. I've talked about practice, games, and fundamentals. There is a lot of material here, and with the information provided here you should be able to take the ideas you're bringing with you and make a good start with your tee ball players. Re-read and review this book often — many of the tips you found here will help in older age groups as well.

As I said, the key is not winning Tee Ball, although you should win if you can. The key is to take your players and teach them as much as you can about the game and the qualities that we like to see in good sportsmen. As you can see from what you've read in this booklet, you have many tools available for you to use in accomplishing these things. If your team wins games as a result of the hard work of everyone involved, so much the better.

I thoroughly enjoyed my time as a Tee Ball manager, coach, and parent and hope that you do too. Good luck!